25 Fun Things to Do for Your NEIGHBORS

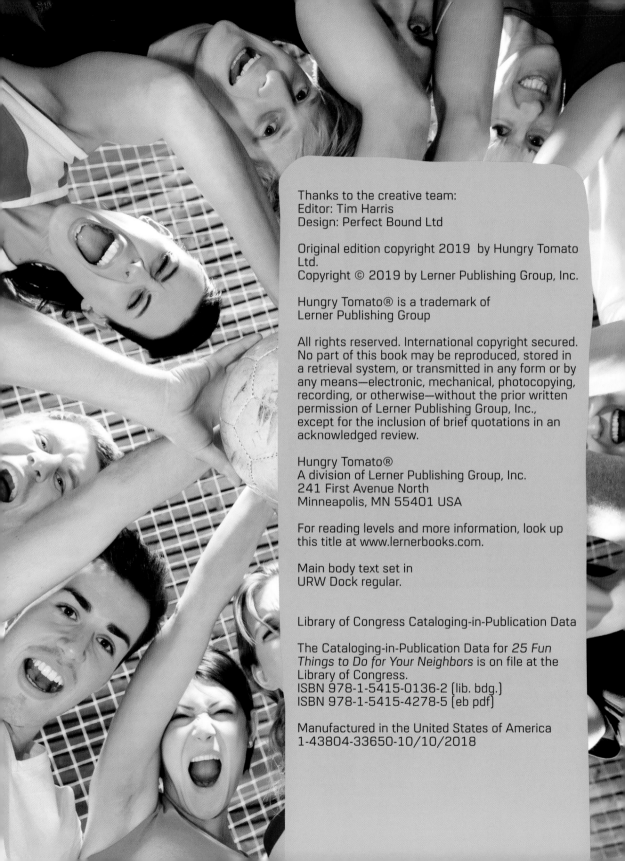

Thanks to the creative team:
Editor: Tim Harris
Design: Perfect Bound Ltd

Original edition copyright 2019 by Hungry Tomato
Ltd.
Copyright © 2019 by Lerner Publishing Group, Inc.

Hungry Tomato® is a trademark of
Lerner Publishing Group

Hungry Tomato®
A division of Lerner Publishing Group, Inc.
241 First Avenue North
Minneapolis, MN 55401 USA

For reading levels and more information, look up
this title at www.lernerbooks.com.

Main body text set in
URW Dock regular.

Library of Congress Cataloging-in-Publication Data

The Cataloging-in-Publication Data for *25 Fun
Things to Do for Your Neighbors* is on file at the
Library of Congress.
ISBN 978-1-5415-0136-2 (lib. bdg.)
ISBN 978-1-5415-4278-5 (eb pdf)

Manufactured in the United States of America
1-43804-33650-10/10/2018

25 Fun Things to Do for Your

NEIGHBORS

PAUL MASON

HUNGRY TOMATO™

MINNEAPOLIS

CONTENTS

Good Neighbors 5

1. Wash a Car 6

2. Vacuum the Interior 7

3. Make Some
Thank-You Cards 8

4. Offer Library Visits 9

5. Oil a Chain 10

6. Adjust Someone's
Bike Gears  11

7. Organize
a Soccer Game 12

8. Clean a Yard 14

9. Take Out the
Trash/Recycling 15

10. Compare Childhoods 16

11. Clean Windows 17

12. Bake a Cake 18

13. Provide Pet Help 20

14. Organize a Kids' Walk 21

15. Have a Street Party 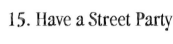 22

16. Grow Some Food
(and Give It Away) 24

17. Give Stuff Away 25

18. Clean Up Trash 26

19. Make an
"I Can Help!" Flyer 27

20. Smile 28

21-25. Five more things… 30

Index 32

Good Neighbors

Living in a neighborhood where people help each other and are friendly makes life better for everyone.

If you are going out to do some good work for your neighborhood, take a friend. It's safer, and whatever job you do will take half as long!

HELPING THOSE WHO CAN'T HELP THEMSELVES

Some of your neighbors might not be able to do things for themselves. For example, someone elderly could find it tricky to reach up and clean their windows. A neighbor who is out at work all day may not be able to walk their dog. A new kid in the neighborhood might not know the way to school yet.

BUILDING YOUR COMMUNITY

If you and your neighbors do things for each other, you get to know them. You might even become friends. Knowing the people who live around you makes life more interesting.

LEARNING

The people who live nearby will know all kinds of things. By helping them, you might be able to learn about gardening, bicycle maintenance, cooking, or lots of other subjects.

STAY SAFE!

If you are ever going into the house of someone you do not know well, make sure one of your parents knows where you are going and has said it's OK. The first time you call on someone new, it would be a good idea to take one of your parents with you.

1. Wash a Car

ALL YOU NEED:

- Big, soft sponge
- Microfiber cloth
- Two buckets
- Watering can or hose
- Soft brush
- Car wash soap

Almost everyone likes it when their car looks clean. Maybe one of your neighbors is not able to wash their car, though. Why not offer to do it for them?

1 **Prepare your cleaning supplies.** Mix a bucketful of warm water and car wash soap, plus another bucket of cold water. Using the watering can or hose, wet the car down. This will soften up dried-on bugs and dirt.

2 **Get washing!** Start at the top with the roof (you may need help from an adult to reach), so that the dirty water runs down over areas you have not washed. Keep rinsing out your sponge in the cold, clean water.

3 **Work your way down.** Next, wash the windows and upper panels. Then go around the hood and lower body panels. The front might need two or three rounds to get all the bugs off. Last, use the brush to clean the wheels.

4 **Rinse and dry.** Use the hose or watering can to rinse the car (again starting at the top). Wipe it dry with the microfiber cloth.

TOP TIP
Don't wash a car in bright sunshine. It dries too quickly and comes out looking smeared.

2. Vacuum the Interior

ALL YOU NEED:

- Vacuum cleaner
- Sponge
- Old toothbrush
- Warm water and dish soap
- Microfiber cloth

The only trouble with a newly washed car is that you cannot see the shine while you are in it. Giving the inside a good clean too will be an even nicer gesture.

1 **Vacuum.** Use the small attachments to vacuum clean the carpets and seats. You can switch to the little brush attachment to clean the dashboard. Be careful, though: the plastic "glass" is easily scratched.

2 **Get nooks and crannies.** Look for tight spaces, like the gap between the driver's seat and the door. These are hard to clean because the vacuum cleaner won't fit. Use a toothbrush to brush out the dirt and vacuum it up.

3 **Clean surfaces.** Wash down hard surfaces using a damp sponge with a TINY bit of dish soap. This will lift off any grease. Use the microfiber cloth rinsed in clean water to wipe the surfaces clean afterward.

BE CAREFUL!
Never clean glass or clear plastic with dish soap. It will get scratched.

3. Make Some Thank-You Cards

ALL YOU NEED:

- Thin cardstock or construction paper
- Regular paper the same size
- Markers, tape, and other decorations
- An envelope

In every neighborhood there are people who do things for the community. Giving them a thank-you card you have made is sure to brighten their day.

1 Decide on a size. How big will your card be? Tiny little cards are nice to get, and so are massive ones. As a start, though, try 4.25 in. x 5.5 in. This is half of a piece of printer paper, folded in half.

2 Practice your design. Before making the actual card, practice on a piece of normal paper. You can do this by folding your paper in half, then in half again.

Your card could be:
- Rainbow stripes
- Polka dot patterns
- A cut-out shape

Or some other design you have come up with.

3 Make the card. Once you are happy with the design, recreate it on the actual card. Don't forget to put a message inside, such as "Thanks for delivering our mail!"

Now put it in the envelope and hand it to the person you want to thank.

4. Offer Library Visits

This is a really easy way to help out a neighbor who finds it tricky to get around—perhaps because they are elderly or have a health problem.

1 **Visit your neighbor.** Go and knock on their door (take your mom or dad with you first time) and explain that you are going to visit the local library. Ask if they would like you to bring them back any books.

2 **Make a list.** Write down the books your neighbor would like. It might be the exact books or a kind of book (spy stories or romances, for example). You might also need to borrow their library card.

3 **Borrow the books.**
Go to the library and borrow the books. If you are just looking for a particular type of book, explain this to the librarian. He or she will give you advice about what to borrow.

4 **Return or renew.** This is an important part: do not forget, the books have to be returned or renewed! Make a note on the calendar of the day before they are due back so you have time to collect them.

5. Oil a Chain

Bicycles with rusty chains are harder to pedal and make a horrible squeaking noise. If you spot a local bike with a rusty chain, you could oil it!

1 **Check the pedals.** You can usually oil a chain without moving the bike. Just carefully move the pedals backward with your hand to make sure you can spin them around without catching them on anything.

   Turning the bike upside down makes this easier.

2 **Drop on the oil.** Slowly turn the pedals backward, adding one drop of oil to each link in the chain. When you get to an oily link, you will know you are back where you started.

3 **Wipe off any extra.** Now put a few drops of oil on your clean cloth. Hold the chain between your thumb and a finger, then slowly move the pedals backward. This spreads the oil out and removes any extra.

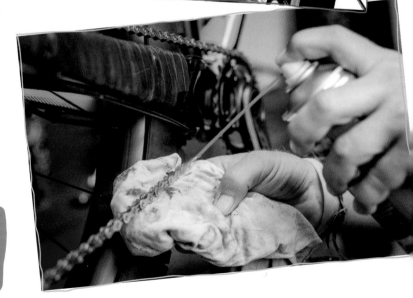

WATCH OUT!
Be very careful not to get your fingers caught while you are oiling or wiping the chain.

6. Adjust Someone's Bike Gears

Sometimes when you are oiling a bike chain (see page 10), the gears keep clanking and getting stuck as you move the pedals. This is a sign there is something else you could do for the owner: adjust their gears.

1 **Turn the bike upside down.** Put the bike upside down, balancing it on its handlebars and seat. Turn the pedals forward and shift the bike into its lowest gear (the smallest cog at the back).

2 **Screw in the adjuster.** Where the gear cable goes into the derailleur (see below), there is a little adjuster that can be screwed in or out. Screw this as far into the derailleur as it will go.

3 **Adjust the gear shift.** Now click the gear shifter once to try and make it go into second gear. Turn the pedals—the gear won't shift.

4 **Get it changing smoothly.** While turning the pedals, start unscrewing the adjuster. The chain will first start to jump, as if it is trying to shift up one gear. Then it will jump across. Unscrew the adjuster a little more, until the chain runs smoothly in second. Job done!

SHOP TALK
Sometimes bikes stop changing gear properly because parts are worn out or damaged. If the tips on this page don't help, the bike might need to go to a bike shop to find out what's wrong.

7. Organize a Soccer Game

A soccer match is a great way for neighbors to get to know each other. On a nice day, try organizing a soccer game for your neighborhood.

1 **Decide who can play.** Your game might be for kids only. Everyone just turns up and you pick teams there.

You could also invite special teams. For example, you could say that teams have to have a certain number of boys and girls, or that the team's total age has to add up to at least 50. For more complicated arrangements like this, people will need more warning.

DOUBLE CHECK
Make sure soccer is allowed at the place you have chosen for the match, as well as that no one else will be using it.

2 **Invite players.** Once you have decided who can play, and when and where the game will be, make some invitations:

You could put invitations through people's doors, pin notices on posts, or do both.

NEIGHBORHOOD SOCCER!

All neighborhood kids invited

When:
This Sunday, June 29

Where:
Barn Walk Playing Fields

3 **Make it a tournament!** If you have enough players, you could make it a tournament with three, four, or five players per team.

8. Clean a Yard

Imagine loving plants but being too elderly or sick to bend down and work in the yard.
If that describes any of your neighbors, cleaning up their yard would be a very good deed indeed.

1 Get permission. First, of course, you need to make sure your neighbor WANTS their yard cleaned up.

Yardwork is much easier with a crew, so it would be a good idea to get some of your friends to come and help too.

2 List your jobs. Make a list with your neighbor of what they would like done. Gardening is hard work, so separate the jobs into one-hour blocks of time:

Hour 1: Clear out dead leaves and fallen branches from flower bed
Hour 2: Water plants with mixture of water and plant food
Hour 3: Use leaf-blower to clear the front driveway and rake leaves into a pile.

TOP TIP

As well as being hard work, gardening can be dirty work, so don't wear your finest fashion gear!

DOUBLE CHECK

If you are cleaning up someone's yard, double-check before cutting down any plants. Chopping down a neighbor's favorite flower bush would NOT be a good deed!

(Always put a fun job at the end—it helps you get through the other ones.)

9. Take Out the Trash/Recycling

This is a good deed you can do for neighbors who find it hard to get around. Elderly people, for example, might find it difficult to carry heavy trash bags.

1 **Get together a client list.** Talk to your parents about whether any of your neighbors might appreciate help with their trash or recycling. Go around to see them and ask.

2 **Take out the trash/recycling.** On the correct day (if there is a collection day where you live), go around and put out the trash/recycling. You could offer to check the recycling to make sure everything is allowed.
If you are moving trash bags, take some spare ones in case any split!

3 **Do a bonus good deed.** Trash is sometimes collected from wheelie bins people leave out on the curb. If you see these have been left out, you could drag them back to your neighbor's property for them.

SCOOPING SNOW
If it is winter and has snowed recently, you may have to clear a spot for the bins!

10. Compare Childhoods

This is a good activity to do with neighbors who were born a long time before you. If you speak to someone who was a child in a different country, their story may be even more interesting.

1 **Pick questions or topics.** Before you speak to your neighbor, think about some of the things that most kids experience. They might include:
- School
- Toys, games, and sports
- Food
- Your bedroom/where you sleep
- Festivals and holidays

   When you speak, these topics might be helpful—you could even turn them into a list of questions.

2 **Write a report.** If you have a school magazine or a neighborhood newsletter, you could write a report about what it was like being a kid in your neighbor's time.

TOP TIP

If you are writing an article, make sure you show it to your neighbor before sending it to anyone else. This gives them a chance to say if they are happy with it and to correct any errors.

11. Clean Windows

Everyone likes having clean windows, but not many people enjoy cleaning them. Window cleaning is a quick, easy job you can do for your neighbors.

ALL YOU NEED:

- An old spray bottle filled with warm water and a squirt of dish soap
- Squeegee
- Bucket of clean, cold water
- Two microfiber cloths

1 **Spray.** Spray the warm, soapy water onto the window, making sure every bit gets wet. Do one window at a time—otherwise some will dry before you get to them.

TOP TIP
Good squeegee technique is the key to good window cleaning! It needs to be angled slightly as you wipe across, so that the wiped-off water trickles down the window.

2 **Squeegee.** Starting at the top of the window, wipe across with the squeegee. Overlap your wipes slightly so that each lower wipe covers the bottom bit of the one above.

3 **Use a wet cloth.** Now use a wrung-out damp microfiber cloth to wipe the whole window clear of smears and marks.

4 **Finish with a dry cloth.** Use your dry cloth to give the window a final polish.

12. Bake a Cake

If you know it's a neighbor's birthday, how about baking them a special surprise? They'll really appreciate it.

ALL YOU NEED:

For the cake:
- 8 in. x 8 in. baking tin
- Parchment paper
- 3 ½ cups of carrots
- ⅞ cup soft brown sugar
- ⅗ cup self-raising flour
- 1 tsp baking soda
- 2 tsp cinnamon
- Zest of an orange
- 2 eggs
- 12 cup sunflower oil

For the icing:
- ½ tbsp. softened butter
- ½ cup powdered sugar
- 6 oz. cream cheese

1 **Prepare.** Line an 8 in. square tin with parchment paper. Preheat the oven to 350°F.

2 **Get grating.** Grate the carrots using the fine side of the grater (the one with the small holes). Next, tip the grated carrot into a big bowl.

3 **Add ingredients.** Using a strainer to make sure there are no lumps, put the sugar, flour, baking soda, and cinnamon on top of the carrot. Next, add the orange zest and mix it all together.

STAY SAFE!

When you are using a grater and an oven, make sure an adult has given you permission or is there to help.

4 **Add eggs.** Break the eggs into a bowl (watch out that no bits of shell get in), then add them and the oil to the other ingredients. Mix everything together well.

5 **Bake!** Pour the mixture into the tin and make sure it is level at the top. Put it in the oven for 30 minutes or until it is brown on top, then take it out and let it cool down.

6 **Make icing.** While the cake is cooking, you can make icing. Mix the butter and powdered sugar together, then stir in the cream cheese until it is all smooth.

7 **Ice, cut, and share.** When the cake is cool, spread icing on top. Cut the cake into squares, ready to share. You could deliver them to your neighbors in little paper bags.

13. Provide Pet Help

ALL YOU NEED:
- Neighbors with pets

If you are someone who likes animals, this is something you can do to help your neighbors that is also a lot of fun.

1 **Offer to help.** You could offer to help in lots of different ways, from walking someone's dog to feeding a cat, or looking after a pet hamster while its owner is on vacation.

DOUBLE CHECK

Before offering to look after someone's pet, speak to your parents and make sure they would be happy for you to take on the job.

2 **Get to know the pet.** If you don't already know it, make sure the pet you are looking after likes you and you like it. Big pets like dogs need to be in control and good at walking on the leash.

3 **Make a list.** With the owner, make a list of the things you need to do to look after their pet:

Horatio the Hamster
- *clean water every morning*
- *give food between 6 and 7 every night*
- *clean out cage Monday, Wednesday, friday*
- *DO NOT allow to escape—he hides!*

HOLD ON!

If you are looking after someone else's dog, never let it off the leash outside—it might run away and not come back!

14. Organize a Kids' Walk

Walking together is a great way to get to know people. There is something about walking that often makes people talkative.

ALL YOU NEED:
- Comfortable shoes
- Small backpack
- Food and drink, or money
- Mobile phone

1 **Plan your route.** It could start with getting everyone. The route could start at one of your homes, then go to the next nearest person's house to get them, the next nearest, and so on.

   Once you have collected everyone, where will you go? Start with a short walk, about 2-3 miles away. This means you will be walking 4-6 miles in total.

2 **Make sure you have enough time.** You will need to make sure you get home in time. But if your walk is 6 miles long, there and back, how long will it actually take you?

   Most people walk at about 3 mph on flat ground. So a 6 mile walk will probably take a bit over 2 hours (especially if you allow some time for breaks).

3 **Draw up a schedule.** Your schedule might look like this:

> 10:30–11:00 Collect walkers
> 11:00 Set off to soccer match
> 12:15 Arrive at soccer pitch
> 12:30–2:30 Watch game
> 2:45 Set off for home
> 4:00–4:30 Drop off walkers

WHERE TO WALK?

Your walk does not have to be in the countryside. You could just as easily walk through town—to a museum, art display, or sports contest, for example.

   If you leave this with a parent, they will know where you are supposed to be and what time to expect you back.

4 **Pack your backpack.** Take something to drink and some food, or money to buy these things if there will be shops to stop in. Take the right clothes too: a wooly hat and sweater if it is cold, or sunscreen and a hat if it is hot.

15. Have a Street Party

A street party for neighborhood kids is a great way to help everyone get to know each other. All you need is a time, some food and drink, and maybe some music.

1 **Get helpers!** Organizing a neighborhood party is a job for a team of people, not just you. Get your friends and parents involved.

2 **Set the time and place.** Decide when the party will be—Halloween or the summer solstice, for example. Put up notices and tell as many other kids as you can find.

Hope for dry weather, because nothing spoils an outdoor party like rain!

3 **Divide jobs.** One person could be in charge of food, with other people doing music playlists, drinks, etc.

Street Party Food: Pinwheel Pizzas

WHAT YOU NEED

For the pizza dough:
- Olive oil
- 3 ½ cups pack bread mix flour
- ½ cup cheddar, grated

For the filling:
- 4 tbsp. pizza sauce
- Handful basil
- 1 whole roasted pepper
- 1 ¼ cups sun-dried tomatoes, chopped up
- 1 cup mozzarella
- 10-in. springform tin

Pinwheel pizzas are a great snack for a street party. They are really easy to make (though you might want a grown-up to help you).

WATCH OUT!

If your party is going to actually block the street, you will need to get permission. Ask your parents to help with this.

1 **Prepare your dough.** Oil a 10-inch springform tin. Make up the bread mix into dough, following the instructions on the packet.

2 **Roll out the dough.** Put the dough on a lightly floured surface, then use a rolling pin to roll it out to roughly 35 x 22 cm.

3 **Add filling.** Spread pizza sauce over the dough, but leave a clear strip around the edge. Scatter the basil, pepper, sun-dried tomato, and mozzarella over the sauce.

4 **Roll it up.** Roll the dough up from the longest side. Now slice it into eight thick pinwheels. Put seven of them around the edge of the tin, with the eighth in the middle. Cover the tin with cling film and leave it in a warm place until it expands and looks much bigger. (This can take up to an hour.)

5 **Cook, cool, and eat.** Heat the oven to 450 ºF. Remove the cling film, sprinkle cheddar cheese on top, and cook for 12-15 minutes until golden. Remove from the oven and let them cool down before eating.

16. Grow Some Food (and Give It Away)

ALL YOU NEED

- Old yogurt container
- Cotton batting
- Paper towel
- Cress seeds
- Water
- Colored markers

Not just any food—you are going to grow Mr. (or Mrs.) Cresshead. This is bound to make your neighbors smile.

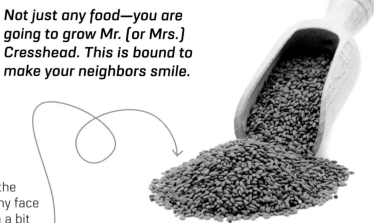

1 **Prepare your pot.** Take the label off and paint a funny face on the front (practice on a bit of scrap paper first). Put wet paper towel at the bottom of the pot, then place some damp cotton batting on top. The cotton batting needs to come almost to the top of the container.

2 **Plant your seeds.** Sprinkle some cress seeds on top of the cotton batting and press them down a bit (not too hard, though).

3 **Position your pot.** Put the pot somewhere sunny and warm, like on a windowsill.

4 **Deliver Mr. (or Mrs.) Cresshead.** After about a week the cress seeds will have grown into green "hair" for Mr. (or Mrs.) Cresshead.
   Now deliver it to one of your neighbors to cut off and put on a sandwich or in some soup!

17. Give Stuff Away

You probably have old toys, clothes, and sports equipment you do not use any more. Maybe some of it would be useful for younger local kids.

1 Work out what you no longer need. Some things are easy. It's impossible to need a coat you have outgrown, for example—it just won't fit you.

With toys and sports equipment, it's harder to decide. Will you really never want a particular game or book again? A good guide is to think when you last used it. If it was over a year ago, you probably don't need it any more.

2 Set up a stand. On a dry day, set up a stand outside your home. You need a little table or a box with the items inside. Add a sign saying "HELP YOURSELF."

If you want to meet the kids who get to use your stuff, you could sit outside and introduce yourself.

DOUBLE CHECK

Before you give anything away, check with your parents first. They might be annoyed if you get rid of something they planned to give to someone else.

HELP YOURSELF

BE 100% POSITIVE

Once you have given something away, you cannot get it back. Make sure you are SURE you won't want it any more.

18. Clean Up Trash

One thing you can do for ALL your neighbors is clean up your neighborhood. On particularly windy days, trash gets blown around and scattered everywhere.

1 **Get a team together.** The more of you there are, the easier the trash pickup will be. Maybe you could get everyone from your walking group (see page 21)—you know they like being outdoors!

2 **Make groups.** You could work in pairs, one with a bag for recyclables and the other for trash. Or there could be three per group, with one person each for paper, plastic, and garbage.

3 **Remove the trash.** The actual garbage needs to go in the trash. If you have found anything containing chemicals, such as old batteries, these usually need to be put in a special waste bin.

The recyclables should go into paper or plastic recycling bins.

4 **Say thank you!** If you want people to help you again, always make sure you thank them for helping this time. As a reward for everyone who helped with the pickup, maybe you could have some of the cake from page 18, or the pinwheel pizzas from page 22.

TRASH DISPOSAL
Check with the local council what you should do with the garbage you find. Plastic, glass, and paper should be recyclable, and sometimes other things are.

19. Make an "I Can Help!" Flyer

ALL YOU NEED

- Paper
- Pencil and markers
- Photocopier or printer

Pick the ideas in this book that you like most. Perhaps you like the idea of dog walking and window cleaning, for example. Make up a flyer to tell people about the things you and your friends can do for them.

1 Decide what to be called.
Maybe you decide to call yourselves Neighbor Angels or Help From the Hood, for example.

2 Add your services.
List the things you can do:

HELP from the HOOD

Dogs walked
Windows cleaned
Mornings, evenings, and weekends
No window too small
(but some are too high...)

We are Pat and Nicki, two local 11-year-olds. If you have jobs you cannot do yourself, we will try to help!

Contact our parents:
hoodhelpers@localmail.com

3 Add a short description.
Say a bit about what you do, who you are, and how to find you. *Always make sure people get in contact through your parents*.

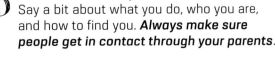

20. Smile

This might be the most important of all the things you can do for your neighbors. It's amazing how much happier life is if people smile at each other—especially if they smile for no particular reason.

YOU COULD . . .

. . . smile when you pass someone on the street

. . . smile at people driving by (and wave if you know them)

. . . smile at people in their yards

In fact, give people a nice smile whenever you get the chance. You are almost certain to get one back!

21-25. Five more things...

There's no need to stop at doing just 20 things for your neighbors—so here are five more!

21 **Eat lunch with a new kid**
Being at a new school can be scary—if you spot a new kid eating alone, sit beside them at lunch to make them feel welcome.

22 **Be an umbrella escort**
On a rainy day at the local store, offer to hold an umbrella over people as they take their shopping back to their car.

23 **Remember birthdays**
Make a little note on the calendar. Everyone loves getting an unexpected birthday card!

24 **Say something nice**
It could just be that you like someone's new haircut, or that their coat looks lovely and warm.

25 **Think . . .**
Think about how your behavior might affect others. For example, is a noisy game a good idea at 6:30 on a Sunday morning, when other people are probably trying to sleep? If you live in an apartment, should you practice your tap dancing at 10:00 on Tuesday night? Probably not!

Index

animals, 20
art display, 21

backpack, 21
ball, 12
bicycle chain, 10–11
books, 9
bowl, 18
bucket, 6, 17

cake, 18, 26
car, 6–7
cat, 20
cloth, 10, 17
community, 5, 8
cooking, 5

derailleur, 11
dog, 20
dog walking, 27
drink, 21–22

elderly person, 5, 9, 15

festivals, 16
food, 21–22, 24

games, 16
gardening, 5, 14
gears, 11
gloves, 14

Halloween, 22
hamster, 20
handlebars, 11

icing, 18
invitations, 13
library, 9

music, 22

newsletter, 16

oil, 10
oven, 18

party, 22
pedals, 10–11
pen, 9
pets, 20
pizza, 22, 26
plants, 14
players, 13

recycling, 15, 26

school, 5, 16
soccer, 13, 21
sports, 16, 25
spy stories, 9

tape, 8
teams, 12
toys, 16, 25
trash, 15

waste, 26
watering can, 6
window cleaning, 5, 17, 27

Picture Credits

THE AUTHOR

Paul Mason is a prolific author of children's books, many award-nominated, on such subjects as how to save the planet, gross things that go wrong with the human body, and the world's craziest inventors. Many include surprising, unbelievable, or just plain disgusting facts. Today, he lives at a secret location on the coast of Europe, where his writing shack usually smells of drying wetsuit (he's a former international swimmer and an enthusiastic surfer).